Amazing Animals
of Oregon

Amazing Animals Series

Amazing Animals of Oregon

INCREDIBLE TRUE STORIES

Gayle C. Shirley

GUILFORD, CONNECTICUT
AN IMPRINT OF THE GLOBE PEQUOT PRESS

To buy books in quantity for corporate use
or incentives, call **(800) 962–0973, ext. 4551,**
or e-mail **premiums@GlobePequot.com.**

INSIDERS' GUIDE®

Copyright © 2005 by The Globe Pequot Press

This book was previously published as *Four-Legged Legends of Oregon* by Falcon Publishing, Inc., in 1995.

All rights reserved. No part of this book may be reproduced or transmitted in any form by any means, electronic or mechanical, including photocopying and recording, or by any information storage and retrieval system, except as may be expressly permitted by the 1976 Copyright Act or by the publisher. Requests for permission should be made in writing to The Globe Pequot Press, P.O. Box 480, Guilford, Connecticut 06437.

Insiders' Guide is a registered trademark of The Globe Pequot Press.

Text design: Nancy Freeborn

Library of Congress Cataloging-in-Publication Data
Shirley, Gayle Corbett.
  Amazing animals of Oregon : incredible true stories / Gayle C. Shirley.—1st ed.
      p. cm.—(Amazing animals series)
  Includes bibliographical references and index.
  ISBN 0-7627-3856-1
  1. Animals—Oregon—Anecdotes. I. Title. II. Series.
  QL201.S55 2005
  591.9795—dc22

                                                        2005014890

Manufactured in the United States of America
First Edition/First Printing

For Megan Hiller, patient and supportive

Contents

Acknowledgments viii

Introduction ix

Seaman: Expedition Mascot 1

Reelfoot: Outlaw Grizzly 11

Bobbie: Cross-Country Canine 19

War Paint: Buckin' Champ 27

Packy: Premier Pachyderm 33

Pete: The Cat's Meow 41

Bob: Forecasting Phenomenon 45

Keiko: Ailing Orca 51

Bibliography 57

About the Author 63

Acknowledgments

I had the help of many generous people while writing *Amazing Animals of Oregon*. For sharing their knowledge, helping to locate research materials, and/or reviewing parts of the manuscript for accuracy, I'd like to thank Mary Appling, Silverton (Oregon) Public Library; Riley Bean, Central Point, Oregon; Mark Berman and other staff at Earth Island Institute, San Francisco, California; Steve Cohen, Metro Washington Zoo, Portland, Oregon; Janice Elvidge and other staff at Fort Clatsop National Memorial, Astoria, Oregon; Mary L. Finney, Pendleton (Oregon) Public Library; Clay Gaillard and other staff at the Professional Rodeo Cowboys Association, Colorado Springs, Colorado; Diane Hammond, Oregon Coast Aquarium, Newport, Oregon; Carol A. Harbison, Southern Oregon Historical Society, Medford, Oregon; Carole Nielson, Shady Cove, Oregon; Shirley Scott, Talent, Oregon; Carol Shiveley, Oregon Humane Society, Portland, Oregon; Jude Smith, Great Falls (Montana) Public Library; Sieglinde Smith, Oregon Historical Society Library, Portland; Jack C. Sweek, Pendleton Round-up Hall of Fame, Pendleton, Oregon; Dick Terwilliger, Siskiyou County Historical Society, Yreka, California; and Gregory Wibe, Multnomah County Library, Portland, Oregon.

And finally, I would especially like to thank my research assistant, Gabriele Sperling, and my husband, Steve Shirley, who shared his editing talent so willingly.

Gayle C. Shirley

Introduction

Ever since man uttered his first words, he's considered himself supreme ruler of the natural world. But he's first and foremost an animal. He can't avoid sharing important, if ambivalent, relationships with the rest of the creatures on earth.

We humans can't help but be fascinated by animals. After all, they're our distant cousins, as well as our companions on the voyage of life. Since the dawn of civilization, we've made them the subjects of our art and folklore. We've worshipped and abused them. We've searched for and celebrated their likenesses to us, but we remain uneasy with their differences.

Author Edith Wharton once wrote in her diary: "I'm secretly afraid of animals. . . . I think it is because of the us-ness in their eyes, with the underlying not-us-ness which belies it, and is so tragic a reminder of the lost age when we human beings branched off and left them . . . to eternal inarticulateness and slavery. 'Why?' their eyes seem to ask us."

■ ■ ■

In *Amazing Animals of Oregon,* you'll get a sense of this love-hate relationship man has with his fellow beings. Most of the animals featured in this book were cherished for their loyalty or admired for their spirit, strength, or intelligence. The grizzly Reelfoot is the exception. He was reviled because his efforts to survive interfered with our own interests. Still, his story reminds us that man's attitude toward animals can change over time. Where once we did our best to exterminate the grizzly, today we afford it special protection to make sure it stays with us in this world—though that doesn't mean our baser instincts no longer exist.

We have mixed feelings, too, about keeping animals in captivity, as illustrated by the stories of Packy the elephant and Keiko the killer whale. As Jean-Michel Cousteau, son of the famous underwater explorer, once said, "We are not gods with a self-bestowed mandate to treat other species as exploitable resources." Is that what we're doing when we confine animals to zoos and aquariums—corralling them for our own amusement? Or are we helping to win them advocates and to ensure the continued existence of their kind? Is it our job to save a species from extinction? By now, we know there are no easy answers. We must continue to explore our motives and weigh our responsibilities to the creatures we walk among.

The stories you're about to read are legends—or, in some cases—legends in the making. Though each tale is true at heart, and though each has been carefully researched and retold as accurately as possible, it's conceivable that a few of the "facts" have been embellished over the years. That, I hope, is excusable. After all, part of the appeal of legends is that they tend to be larger than life.

The animals featured here were selected because they demonstrated that they were special. They captured our imagination. All of them achieved some measure of fame not only in Oregon but nationwide. Because we thought them unique, we gave them names, and we've kept their legends alive. Even with the passage of decades, their stories still stir our hearts.

"The animal[s] shall not be measured by man. . . . They are not brethren, they are not underlings; they are other nations, caught with ourselves in the net of life and time, fellow prisoners of the splendor and travail of the earth."

Henry Beston
The Outermost House

Statue of Seaman in Seaside, Oregon. David B. Hunsaker photo

Seaman
Expedition
Mascot

"[Seaman] is part of our country's history.
With fidelity and courage, he partici-
pated in an historic event which had a
profound effect on our nation's future.
He [was] true to the pact made eons ago
between man and dog."

—ERNEST S. OSGOOD, *Montana, the Magazine of Western History,*
Summer 1976

The members of the Lewis and Clark Expedition were
eager to leave Fort Clatsop on that dull, soggy day in March
1806. For three and a half miserable months, they'd waited
out the winter at their makeshift camp at the mouth of the
Columbia River in what is now northwestern Oregon. Fre-
quent rains had spoiled their food and their health. Fleas had
tormented them. Their tobacco supply was nearly gone, and
there wasn't even any whiskey left with which to drown
their sorrows.

Now at last, almost two years after setting out to explore the mysterious wilderness west of the Mississippi River, the haggard heroes were on their way home!

The return trip got off to a wet and turbulent start. It continued to rain often, drenching the men and swelling the Columbia until, in Lewis's estimation, it was about 12 feet higher than it had been on their westward journey to the Pacific Ocean. The men strained to paddle their canoes upsteam through high winds and heavy waves.

To make matters worse, there was very little food. The salmon had not yet begun their spring spawning run up the Columbia, and the elk had already moved to their summer ranges high in the coastal mountains. Members of the expedition would have to settle for a diet of roots and dog meat, obtained through trade with the local Indians.

The famished explorers soon got over any reluctance they might have had about eating "man's best friend." Captain Meriwether Lewis confessed in his journal that: "dog now constitutes a considerable part of our subsistence and with most of the party has become a favorite food; certain I am that it is a healthy strong diet, and from habit it has become by no means disagreeable to me, I prefer it to lean venison or Elk, and it is very far superior to the horse in any state."

■ ■ ■

This was not to say that Lewis only liked dogs as part of the daily menu. In fact, the Captain kept a dog as a pet—a large, black Newfoundland named Seaman. The animal had come along on the expedition to serve as a hunter and sentry.

- 2 -

By mid-April of 1806, the explorers had traveled about two hundred miles upriver and had reached the chaotic rapids known as the Cascades. Unable to paddle through them, the men attached ropes to their canoes and towed the craft through, scrambling alongside on the rocky shore. Some Indians—called Wahclellahs by Lewis—crowded the riverbank to watch the tedious task. According to the Captain, "one of them had the insolence to cast stones down the bank at two of the men who happened to be a little detached from the party at the time."

Relations with some of the American Indian tribes in the Columbia Valley had lately been a bit strained. Although many of the Indians had been peaceable and had sold food and firewood to the expedition, some had also occasionally helped themselves to the explorers' belongings. At least one of the members of the Corps considered the Wahclellahs a "tribe of villains," and they had a reputation as expert thieves.

On the evening of April 11, three Wahclellah men attempted a heist that pushed Lewis to the limits of his patience. They kidnapped Seaman, perhaps with the intention of adding him to a stew. For this one time only, the Captain disregarded his orders to maintain friendly relations with the Indians along his route.

He recorded his ruthless reaction to the theft in his journal later that night: "I . . . sent three men in pursuit of the theives [sic] with orders if they made the least resistance or difficulty in surrendering the dog to fire on them; they overtook these fellows or reather [sic] came within sight of them at the distance of about 2 miles; the Indians discovering the party in pursuit of them left the dog and fled. We . . . informed them by signs that if they made any further attempts to steal our property or insulted our men we should put them to instant death."

■ ■ ■

Clearly, Seaman meant a great deal to his master—and for good reason. Many times during the explorers' 4,000-mile trek across the continent, the dog had proved to be loyal, brave, and strong, a good hunter and sentinel—in short, a valuable member of the expedition. He had even saved his master's life, turning aside a stampeding bison bull that was about to trample Lewis and William Clark as they slept. Seaman was all anyone could ask for in a dog—and more.

Lewis bought his Newfoundland for twenty dollars, probably during the preparation for the Voyage of Discovery. The good-natured breed was popular at the time, especially with the crews of ocean-going ships. Because of its water-resistant coat, webbed toes, and great size and strength, it took readily to water and could rescue sailors swept overboard into the icy sea. In fact, the dog was believed to have natural life-saving instincts—a trait that Lewis would have found attractive.

Author Louis Charbonneau, who researched the breed for *Trail*, his novel about the Lewis and Clark Expedition, concluded that Seaman probably didn't look like the Newfoundlands of today. In fact, he said: "he would have been a leaner, rangier dog, his muzzle a little longer and not as deep, and without as pronounced a stop. . . . He was probably black with a distinctive white star on his chest. Although many Newfoundlands of the time were parti-colored . . . the black dogs were more highly prized, and Lewis's dog was almost certainly one of them."

- 4 -

■ ■ ■

For almost two centuries, historians believed that Lewis named his dog Scannon. Then, in 1985, historian Donald Jackson made an unexpected discovery. While studying the way Lewis and Clark chose names for the geographic features they encountered, Jackson was perplexed to find that Lewis had given the name Seaman's Creek (now Monture Creek) to a tributary of the Blackfoot River in Montana.

He accounted for this oddity in *Among the Sleeping Giants: Occasional Pieces on Lewis and Clark:* "No person named Seaman is known to have been associated with the lives of either captain, and as a common term the word seemed strangely out of place in Montana. . . . The thought occurred to me that the name might be a garbled version of Scannon's Creek, to commemorate the dog. . . . But when I consulted microcopies of the journals . . . what I learned instead was mildly startling: the stream was named Seaman's Creek because the dog's name was Seaman."

■ ■ ■

As Jackson went on to point out, ink has a way of spreading over the years, so that an *e* might fill in to resemble the letter *c* and a *m* might be misread as *nn*. To a person aware of the correct name, it fairly jumps from the journals of the Expedition. Certainly, Seaman was a logical name for a dog who by nature was at home in the water.

Lewis first mentioned Seaman in his journal almost a full year before the expedition officially began. On August 30, 1803, after a series of frustrating delays, Lewis and a party of about eleven men finally left Pittsburgh and headed down the Ohio River to the Missouri. One hundred miles downstream, Lewis noticed a number of squirrels swimming the river. "I made my dog take as many each day as I had occasion for," he wrote. ". . . I thought them when fryed [*sic*] a pleasant food." He would discover later that Seaman was capable of landing much larger game.

At the junction of the Ohio and Mississippi rivers, Lewis and his party met a group of Shawnees and Delawares living on the west bank of the Mississippi. One of the Shawnees took a fancy to Seaman and offered Lewis three beaver pelts for him. But Lewis prized the dog for his "docility and qualifications generally" for the journey, and so "of course there was no bargain."

The men of the expedition spent the winter near the junction of the Mississippi and Missouri Rivers. Finally, on May 14, 1804, the party that Clark described as "46 men, 4 horses, and 1 dog" headed up the Missouri, launching one of the great adventures of all time. Four thousand miles and eighteen months or rivers and trails lay between them and the Pacific Ocean.

The trials and tribulations of the Lewis and Clark Expedition are well known, and Seaman shared in them all. Not the least of these torments was the mosquitoes, especially at the Great Falls of the Missouri in what is now Montana. "My dog even howls with the torture he experiences from them," Lewis wrote.

Yet another affliction was the prickly pear cactus. Its sharp spines pierced the men's moccasins, as well as the pads of Seaman's paws. "My poor dog suffers with them excessively," Lewis noted. "He is constantly biting and scratching himself as if in a rack of pain."

But Seaman did more than endure hardships. He also made his own contributions to the success of the expedition.

- 6 -

He was a skillful hunter capable of chasing down deer and swimming to shore with antelope and beaver he drowned in the river. He could even dive underwater and drag the latter out of their lodges. Those squirrels on the Ohio had just been a warm-up!

Hunting beaver almost proved fatal to Seaman on one occasion. Lewis reported that "my dog as usual swam in to catch it; the beaver bit him through the hind leg and cut the artery; it was with great difficulty that I could stop the blood; I fear it will yet prove fatal to him."

But Seaman was made of stronger stuff than Lewis realized. Only nine days later, the dog valiantly protected his master from the sharp hooves of the stampeding bison, which had blundered into their camp along the Missouri River in present-day Montana.

Among the Indians, Seaman proved as great a curiosity as York, Clark's black servant. The big dog must have looked to them like a small black bear with floppy ears and a wagging tail. To some of the Wahclellahs, at least, he was irresistible.

Seaman is last mentioned in the expedition journals on July 15, 1806, when Lewis complained about the mosquitoes at the Great Falls. Yet the party still had about 1,600 miles to cover before reaching home. Did the expedition's loyal mascot finish the journey to St. Louis? Or did his luck run out somewhere along the way? Historian Ernest S. Osgood pondered those questions and reached his own conclusion.

On July 17, Osgood noted, Lewis and three of his men separated from the rest of the party to explore the curse of the Marias River in what is now Montana. Ten days later, they took part in the only fatal skirmish with Indians or the entire voyage. The four men had encountered eight Blackfeet and camped with them along the South Fork of the

- 7 -

Marias, now called the Two Medicine. At daybreak, the Blackfeet tried to steal the explorers' guns, and a struggle ensued. Two warriors were killed. The rest of the Blackfeet fled, and Lewis decided it would be prudent if he and his party rejoined their comrades "as quick as possible." They forced their horses and themselves to near exhaustion, covering about 120 miles in twenty-four hours. Was Seaman with them? wondered Osgood.

"We know that 'our dog' was an alert, vigilant and courageous guard. Would he not have raised an alarm the moment those Indians got up to steal the guns? Would he have allowed an Indian to approach his sleeping master . . . ? If [Seaman] were with his master . . . it would have been impossible for him to keep up with the horses who were pushed to the limits of their endurance. Left alone on those empty plains with such predators as the wolves and grizzlies on the prowl, [Seaman's] fate would have been sealed."

■ ■ ■

Osgood suggests a more palatable scenario: Maybe Lewis didn't take Seaman along to the Marias but left him instead with Clark and the others when the two leaders parted at the Great Falls.

Author Charbonneau arrived at a different conclusion about Seaman's fate. In his opinion, Lewis did take his dog with him when he set off for the Marias. The Captain was heading into hostile Indian territory and would have been glad to have an additional camp guard. Then, when he and his men fled for their lives after the clash with the Blackfeet, they had no choice, in Charbonneau's view, but to abandon their gallant pet.

- 8 -

But a week and 350 miles later, Lewis and his party stopped for a couple of days to dry out their belongings and do some hunting. Could Seaman have caught up with them?

According to Charbonneau: "it meant that Seaman would have had to travel overland between fifty and sixty miles a day for seven days (allowing for detours) across a prairie teeming with buffalo, bears, and wolf packs. Was that truly beyond the capacity of a big dog toughened by three years on the trail? One who had easily kept up with Lewis and his party less than a month earlier when they crossed the mountains from Traveler's Rest on horseback, routinely covering over thirty miles a day? Was he capable of surviving the perils along the way? Did he have the strength, intelligence and determination that would enable him once more to see his companions . . . ?"

■ ■ ■

In Charbonneau's opinion, Seaman did.

The fact that Lewis's dog is never mentioned in the expedition journals after July 15, 1806, doesn't mean that he was killed or lost. In fact, it may indicate otherwise, since it seems likely Lewis would have mentioned the loss of his loyal companion. Both Charbonneau and Osgood concluded that Seaman was with the expedition when it arrived at St. Louis on September 23, 1806. Given the courage and loyalty with which Seaman served his master, one can't help but embrace this upbeat ending to the canine adventurer's story.

- 9 -

Reelfoot. Siskiyou County Museum, Yreka, California

Reelfoot
Outlaw Grizzly

"Many years have passed since grizzly bears roamed the forest of southern Oregon . . . , but the memory of Reelfoot still lingers. Tales of his great size, immense strength, his ability to outwit the human schemes to kill him, coupled with his uncanny instincts, are told wherever old timers meet."

—GEORGE F. WRIGHT, "The Truth about Reelfoot"

J. D. Williams roamed the foothills of the Siskiyou Mountains, tending his sheep on a tranquil spring day in 1882. The scene was as pastoral as a Constable painting: Williams's herd drifted before him like cumulus clouds before a slight breeze, and in a meadow below, a handful of cattle grazed under the watchful eye of a large and sinewy bull. All it took to destroy Williams's peace of mind was the sight of a fresh pawprint in the earth at his feet. It was the track of a gigantic grizzly, and

- 11 -

its maker, the shepherd now saw, was lurking in the timber at the edge of the glade.

Williams felt his insides cramp with fear. He had left his rifle in camp that morning, so he scrabbled up a nearby tree, stopping only when the branches threatened to break under his weight. Then, from the safety of his perch, he watched a deadly drama unfold below.

The bear paid no attention to Williams but focused instead on the unsuspecting cattle. Before the herd realized it was in danger, the grizzly burst from its cover and attacked, killing a calf that grazed at its mother's side. The cow tried to defend her offspring, but the silvertip slew her, too, with one swipe of its steely claws.

With a bellow, the bull counterattacked. He lowered his head and charged, slamming the grizzly to the ground, but it lurched to its feet again with a bawl of pain and rage and lunged for its attacker, ripping and tearing with teeth and claws. The bull fought back, slashing with his horns and gouging with his hooves. For what seemed to Williams like an eternity, the two creatures grappled in a blur of blood, fur, dirt, and drool.

Finally, the grizzly clamped its powerful jaws around the bull's nose and, with a wrench, snapped the animal's neck. The bull slumped to the ground and lay in a grotesque heap. The victor gorged on the calf and enjoyed a brief wallow in a mudhole before sauntering away.

Williams didn't budge until long after the bear was gone. When he did climb down and inspect its curious tracks, he realized with a shudder that he had just encountered Reelfoot, the most infamous predator on the Oregon-California border.

Grizzlies had roamed the rugged Siskiyou Mountains long before pioneers began pouring into the region's fertile valleys and turning livestock loose to graze. Inevitably, the bears began to prey on these growing herds, but the stockmen fought back, hunting, trapping, and poisoning the predators until their numbers dwindled dramatically. Nonetheless, settlers continued to find the mutilated bodies of cattle, sheep, and horses littering the range, and by the 1870s, it had become clear that one monstrous bear was primarily to blame.

The Grieve brothers, who ranched along the Klamath River, were among the many who had lost stock to the marauder. They tried repeatedly to trap the bear, and on one occasion they almost succeeded. Bruce Grieve had set a trap beside the partially devoured carcass of one of his heifers, in the hope the killer would return to feast again. When he checked the trap later, he found that it had, indeed, been sprung, but his quarry had escaped, leaving only three toes from its left front paw clenched in the brutal jaws. From then on, stockmen in Oregon called the grizzly Reelfoot, because of its uneven gait, while in California they dubbed him Clubfoot. His name became synonymous with terror and destruction on both sides of the border, and settlers dreaded the sight of his telltale tracks.

For the next two decades, Reelfoot ruled a vast domain that covered Jackson and Klamath counties in Oregon and Siskiyou County in California. He killed, ate, and moved on, leaving a trail of carnage behind him. Even his method of killing was distinctive. He would rush his prey and knock it to the ground, then crush its spine with one snap of his jaws.

As Reelfoot's reputation grew, cattlemen grew more desperate to stop him. A rancher near Ashland posted a $500 reward for the grizzly's death, nailing the notice to the trunk of a pine. Others tacked up their own pledges, until the tree fluttered with a mantle of paper leaves, and the bounty for

Reelfoot had swelled to more than $2,000—an inspiring sum back in those days. Soon the silvertip's trail was overrun with the footsteps of would-be heroes who vowed to pin his hide to their cabin walls.

But Reelfoot was a crafty creature and had learned from his painful encounter with Grieve's trap. He rarely returned to a kill after his first meal now, and he had an uncanny knack for eluding pursuers. Bill Wright, a Siskiyou County rancher, conceived what he thought was a foolproof plan to kill the bear. He hung some meat from a tree and rigged it to his rifle in such a way that the bear would be shot if he tried to take the bait. But Reelfoot simply stood on his hand legs behind the tree and reached around it to snag the meat. The gun went off, but the bullet lodged harmlessly in the tree trunk.

On another occasion, Reelfoot killed several sheep at a camp near Hornbrook, California, only one of which he bothered to eat. A hunting party tracked the outlaw for more than a hundred miles, from Hornbrook all the way to Crater Lake, without ever catching a glimpse of him. Finally, footsore and bone-weary, they gave up and went home. In the next three days, Reelfoot slaughtered fifteen sheep, a calf, and a sheep dog, all in the vicinity of Hornbrook. It seemed almost as if he had committed the deeds just to spite his pursuers.

By April 1890, Reelfoot stood accused of killing hundreds of head of livestock and of baffling even the most experienced hunters and trappers. But he was about to meet his nemesis—in the form of Bill Wright and a seventeen-year-old neighbor named Purl Bean.

According to some accounts, Wright took to Reelfoot's trail after watching helplessly as the grizzly killed his prize bull while it grazed near the homesteader's cabin. But Wright's nephew, George, grew up hearing a different story. He claimed his uncle decided to hunt the bear after it killed a cow belonging to a neighbor. Whatever the reason, Wright set out with Bean and three other hunters on April 5, 1890, determined to put a stop to Reelfoot's rampage.

For four days, the hunters stalked the bear through thick brush and deep snow in wild, rough mountain country. Although they came across fresh tracks, they never saw the silvertip, so they gave up and went home, weary and discouraged.

The next day, April 10, Wright decided to try again. This time, he took with him only a pack of hunting dogs and Bean, who, despite his youth, had a reputation as a crack shot. On foot, the pair followed the tracks of the rogue bear up Camp Creek and into the heart of the jagged Siskiyous. Suddenly, about three miles south of Pilot Rock, they spotted their quarry in a brushy, snow-choked draw.

Wright's nephew described the gruesome encounter that followed:

> The bear . . . had just gotten up from his bed, made on a flattened wood-rat's nest. . . . The hunters were standing on a hillside, about one hundred feet from the little gulch. They both at once fired . . . at a distance of about one hundred and twenty five yards as the bear left his bed; bullets took effect As soon as [the bear was] shot he showed fight and made for the hunters, tearing up with his teeth large shrubs and brush in his anger, and fighting the two dogs as he came. Blended with the rifle fire was the barking of the two dogs and the roaring growls of an enraged, huge grizzly bear. The hunters stood their

- 15 -

ground, to kill or be killed, taking good aim and firing as fast as possible and with good effect. By this time the bear had fought his way down to the bottom of the gulch, where the dogs "bayed" him for a few minutes, giving the hunters time to reload their repeating rifles.

Although the bear showed some signs of weakening, the dogs were tired also. The men agreed that Wright would shoot for [Reelfoot's] head, and Bean for the heart. With their rifles fully loaded again they started firing; still the weakened bear fought his way up the hillside of the gulch, trying to get at his assailants. When within forty feet of the men, the great bear unexpectedly toppled over dead. Thus ended the career of this much feared and noted grizzly. The hunters probably breathed a sigh of relief. . . .

■ ■ ■

Using his 9-inch hunting knife as a measuring stick, Bean sized up the bear. The rogue was said to be 8 feet long from nose to tail, with 4½-inch claws. He was estimated to weigh anywhere from 1,800 to 2,250 pounds—two or three times as much as the average grizzly and even more than the largest bear in *The Guinness Book of World Records!* The hunters also counted ten bullet holes in the silvertip's hide. Death had not come easy to Reelfoot.

Wright and Bean hired a taxidermist to mount the infamous grizzly. Then they loaded him into a wagon and exhibited him in towns throughout western Oregon and northern California, charging curiosity seekers ten cents a look. Eventually, the hunters sold their trophy, apparently to a Dr. Jordan.

What really happened to Reelfoot next is a mystery. Some say that he was purchased by the Native Sons of the Golden West to be displayed in their headquarters in San Francisco, and that he was destroyed in the fire and earthquake that leveled much of the city in 1906. Others say he was featured at the 1893 World's Fair in Chicago. And at least one soldier returning from overseas duty during World War I claimed to have seen him in a London museum.

In the late 1930s, a Hornbrook man named Gordon Jacobs tried and failed to locate the mounted bear for exhibit in the Siskiyou County Museum in Yreka, California. For several years, the museum displayed the claws pried from Bruce Grieve's trap, but even those grisly mementos have disappeared—just as grizzlies have disappeared from the Siskiyou Mountains.

Today, all that remains of Reelfoot are a handful of fading photos and a tantalizing tale.

Bobbie, the "Wonder Dog of Oregon." Oregon Humane Society

Bobbie
Cross-Country
Canine

"It is wonderful to think that a lower animal entertains for his master an affection so sincere that he will trudge friendless over prairies and mountain ranges until at length his dusty, burning nostrils catch the green, glad scent of home."

—EDITORIAL in *The Sunday Oregonian,* April 10, 1927

Dust-covered and travel-weary, Frank Brazier nosed his new touring car into the curb outside a friend's house in Wolcott, Indiana. For the past ten days, he and his wife, Elizabeth, had endured a bone-rattling ride over 2,500 miles of rutted dirt road, wilting in the glare of the late-summer sun. Now, finally, they had reached the first stop of their ambitious cross-country vacation.

The Braziers had left their home in Silverton, Oregon, on August 6, 1923, to visit friends and relatives in the Midwest. With them, they had brought their dog, Bobbie, a stub-tailed, two-year-old mongrel with a large dose of collie and

– 19 –

a smidgen of sheep dog coursing through its veins. He spent the long trip perched on top of the luggage in the back seat or riding into the wind. Sometimes, when the Braziers stopped to eat, he would scamper after a rabbit and return an hour or so later, panting and grinning about his adventure.

By Wolcott, the Braziers' car was feeling its mileage, so Frank left his wife at their friend's house and drove to a local garage for a once-over and a tank of gas. He was inside talking to a mechanic when he heard Bobbie yelp in pain. He rushed out to see his dog bolting down the street with a pack of snarling, snapping curs at his heels.

Frank was fond of his shaggy mutt, but he also figured Bobbie was tough enough to fend for himself, so he went back into the garage to wait until his car was ready. He expected to find his dog waiting for him at the friend's house when he returned. But hours passed with no sign of Bobbie, and Frank began to get alarmed. He decided to take a drive around Wolcott, honking his car's distinctive horn. It had never yet failed to bring his dog running.

But this time, Bobbie didn't respond. At midnight, Frank finally gave up his search and, heart sinking, went to bed. The next morning, he canvassed the small farm town by phone, hoping someone had seen his furry friend. He even placed an ad in the local newspaper, offering a reward. But all his efforts were in vain. His dog, it seemed, had simply vanished.

Finally, the Braziers had no choice but to move on. Resigning themselves to the loss of their beloved pet—as well as their holiday spirit—they continued on with their vacation, motoring around Indiana, into Ohio, and then home via Mexico and the Southwest. Back in Silverton, they broke the sad news to their two teenage daughters that Bobbie had disappeared.

Exactly six months later, the younger Brazier girl, Nova, was walking down South Water Street with a chum when she noticed a thin, pathetic dog limping along the sidewalk.

"Oh, look!" she exclaimed, seizing her friend by the arm. "Isn't that Bobbie?"

Her father later described the touching reunion that followed: "At the words, a shaggy, bedraggled, lean dog just beyond them turned his head and the next moment fairly flew at Nova, leaping up again and again to cover her face with kisses and making half-strangled, sobbing sounds of relief and delight as if he could hardly voice his wordless joy. It was Bobbie, sure enough, and it was a glad and triumphant procession which hurried on to the restaurant, where the dog hunted out my wife and [daughter] Leona, and told them how happy he was to be home again. But there was someone else he wanted to see. Paying no attention to the crowd of curious and sympathetic bystanders, he rushed through the rooms in search of me. As I take charge of things at night [at the restaurant owned by the Braziers], I was sleeping upstairs, and was awakened by a whirlwind which burst in at my door, composed of my excited wife and dog. 'Look who's here,' she cried. I could not believe my eyes. But it was no dream, for a wet tongue lapping feverishly at my face and two dirty paws resting on my shoulders told me it was not a ghost, but Bobbie sure enough, who had miraculously returned."

■ ■ ■

For the next three days, Bobbie did little but eat and sleep. His toenails were worn to the quick, the pads of his paws were bruised and bleeding, and his coat was matted and

– 21 –

filthy—all evidence of his having survived a terrible ordeal. Skeptics suggested this was just some look-alike stray, but the scars of three old injuries convinced the Braziers that this was, indeed, their Bobbie. But how, they marveled, could he have found his way home across 2,500 miles of unfamiliar territory? What mysterious sixth sense had guided him across rivers, prairies, and mountain ranges right to his own front door?

It wasn't until years later that the Braziers were able to piece together Bobbie's odyssey. As the story of his poignant homecoming made headlines across the nation, the family began to get letters from people claiming to have seen the dog in the course of his epic journey. Eventually, the Braziers were able to establish a chronology of their pet's homeward trip.

No one knows how or where Bobbie survived the first few weeks of his ordeal, but almost a month after fleeing the Wolcott garage, he appeared on the doorstep of a hardware clerk in Wolcottville, Indiana, about 100 miles to the northeast. Bobbie stayed with the clerk for about a week, resting and regaining his strength. Then he set off again on his lonesome quest for home.

Next, a group of hobos noticed Bobbie swimming across the White River just outside Indianapolis. When the soggy stray hauled himself ashore, the men offered to share their meal of stew and crackers with him. He spent a couple of days tagging along with the sympathetic drifters and then, again, he moved on.

The next person known to have seen Bobbie was a woman who was sitting under a tree beside the Wabash River when she saw a dog crawl out of the water. Moved by his pitiful condition, she took him home and fed him, hoping he would stay. But the next day, much to her dismay, he moved on.

- 22 -

Bobbie turned westward and trotted across Illinois into Iowa. One autumn day, he was headed through the town of Vinton when he heard the familiar bleat of a car horn. Pulse quickening, he leaped into the open car expecting a welcome hug from his master, but he landed instead in the laps of a passel of strangers. The family, whose car it was, later told how startled they were by the bob-tailed collie. They sheltered him for the night, but in the morning he moved on.

Shortly before Thanksgiving, Bobbie straggled into Des Moines and crept onto a porch where a young boy was sleeping. The pair nestled together for the night, closing ranks against the chill, and were discovered in the morning by the boy's surprised aunt. Bobbie must have liked the family, because he stayed with them for several weeks. Every day he would go out for a few hours to search the city for signs of his master, but all he found was a cunning dogcatcher who later vividly recalled cornering the scrappy stray only to watch in dismay as it escaped by leaping over him.

So far, Bobbie seemed to have been roaming aimlessly, with no clear idea of his bearings. But at the end of November, after his run-in with the dogcatcher, some slumbering instinct suddenly stirred. He bolted westward as surely as a sailor guided by Polaris and arrived in Denver, Colorado— 500 miles distant—only six days later. On the way, he narrowly escaped being caught by a Missouri River bridge guard. He dodged the man by diving into the icy water and paddling his way to the western shore. In Denver, he briefly found refuge with yet another Good Samaritan.

From Colorado, Bobbie headed northwestward, skirting the snow-clogged Rocky Mountains and working his way into Wyoming. There, a sheepherder found him huddled at the door of his hut one day and recognized in him a potential herd dog. Bobbie repaid the man's hospitality the very next night, when a blizzard threatened to wipe out seven thousand panicky sheep. The man later credited Bobbie with turning the herd away from the edge of a cliff and driving them to safety. Eventually, though, the dog moved on.

Bobbie was reportedly sighted next at a livery stable in western Wyoming, where he hooked up for a few days with a greenhorn lawyer who had stopped to buy a horse. A few days later, a rancher found the feeble animal caught in one of his traps. The man was so taken with the dog that he decided to keep him, but Bobbie had other ideas and, about a week later, he moved on.

Somehow, Bobbie picked his way through Idaho, crossing the Snake, Salmon, and Payette Rivers. In January, he reached Oregon and wandered into the Columbia River Valley. He headed westward via the Columbia Highway, stopping briefly in The Dalles for another charitable meal.

By now, Bobbie was in the home stretch, only a few hundred miles from Silverton. He turned southward and bypassed Portland, but in East Portland his journey almost came to an untimely end. Dazed, famished, and exhausted, he collapsed at the door of an Irish widow, who carried him inside to die. She sang him lullabies, bathed his sores, coated his feet with soothing ointment, and spoonfed him water because he was too weak to eat on his own. It nearly broke her heart, when, the next morning, he hobbled stiffly to her front door and whimpered for his freedom. But she let him go, and he moved on.

Only 70 miles now lay between Bobbie and home, but wasted as he was, it took him two weeks to negotiate them. He padded into Silverton exactly six months to the day after his disappearance in Indiana, and somehow he summoned the strength for his exuberant family reunion. All told, with wrong turns included, Bobbie had traveled about 3,000 miles across eight states to find his hearth and home—all with nothing to guide him but instinct and a heart full of love.

People everywhere were deeply moved by the story of Bobbie's undying devotion. The Oregon Humane Society awarded him a silver medal engraved with the record of his prodigious journey. The Portland Realty Board invited him to be an honored guest at the city's week-long home show, where an estimated 50,000–60,000 people viewed and petted him. Bobbie was so popular that police were hired and a wire fence erected to protect him from the adoring crowds. He went home at the end of the week with two distinguished gifts: a silver-plated collar and a custom-made, dog-sized bungalow complete with glass windows, silk curtains, and a solid oak door.

In a matter of weeks, Bobbie became a tongue-lolling, tail-wagging, international celebrity. The mayors of Silverton and Portland awarded him the keys to their cities, and admirers from as far away as England, France, and Australia showered him with gifts and fan mail addressed simply to "Bobbie the Wonder Dog, Silverton, Oregon." His odyssey was celebrated in at least two movies and a pair of books, as well as in *Ripley's Believe It or Not*. He still holds the Guinness record for the longest tracking ever accomplished by a dog.

There was, indeed, much to admire in Bobbie's incredible cross country adventure. There was his physical courage in the face of hunger, bitter cold, exhaustion, and prowling predators. And there was the inexplicable instinct that guided him home from halfway across the continent.

But what impressed people the most about Bobbie's feat was its emotional appeal—the way it tugged at their heartstrings. For what man, woman, or child could fail to admire such selfless devotion as Bobbie had for his master—a devotion so true that he refused to give up his quest, despite countless hurdles thrown his way?

"A man thus lost and bewildered, would have resigned himself to new friends and forgotten the old," wrote Charles Alexander, in his book *Bobbie: A Great Collie.* "This is the virtue of splendid dogs, that they give loyalty and faith beyond man's understanding. . . . Something of decidedly heroic stature clings about [Bobbie's story], something inadmissible that should not be let slip into oblivion."

Bobbie died peacefully on April 6, 1927, and canine movie star Rin Tin Tin was among the dignitaries who attended his funeral. Bobbie was buried in the pet cemetery of the Oregon Humane Society, where visitors can still see a replica of Bobbie's well-appointed doghouse today and a mural devoted to his inspiring story. Bobbie's legacy has been so lasting that in 2004 the Silverton Market Garden erected a handsome bronze bust of him at the head of a raised pool fountain.

War Paint
Buckin' Champ

"A horse is born to buck—it's natural—
but some are better than others."

—BOBBY CHRISTENSEN JR.

Cowboy hats bobbled like whitecaps on the sea of spectators waiting for the rodeo event of the year: an exhibition match pitting champion against champion. A moment ago, the crowd at the Denver Coliseum had watched as one of the contenders—an Oregon-born pinto gelding—had trotted docilely into the area, looking a bit shaggy in his long winter coat. Now, the audience applauded politely as the other—a North Dakota cowboy—stepped into the spotlight looking, as one observer said, like "a country kid dressed up for a 4-H Club dance."

The cowboy, Alvin Nelson, grinned and doffed his hat as he was introduced to the crowd at the National Western Rodeo on that January evening in 1958. Meanwhile, only about a dozen yards behind him, a team of rodeo hands loaded the brown and white pinto, War Paint, into one of the bucking chutes. The newly proclaimed world champion saddle

Harry Nobel rides War Paint in Klamath Falls, Oregon, 1960. Pendleton Round-Up & Happy Canyon Hall of Fame

bronc rider of 1957 was about to take on the top bucking horse of the year.

As the ceremony ended, Nelson shrugged off his suit jacket and buckled on his royal blue chaps. He deserved the championship belt buckle he had just won. He had recently finished a six-month winning streak unrivaled in rodeo, placing at every major event he entered and winning $18,000 in prize money.

As he climbed the gate of the chute, the crowd grew as quiet as a bunkhouse on a Saturday night. Even the guys hawking soda pop and candy swallowed their sales pitches and watched in silence. Nelson eased down into the saddle, slipped the toes of his boots into the stirrups, and squeezed the coarse, braided rope rein with one hand. War Paint stood relaxed and steady, too wise to waste his energy struggling in the chute.

As the gate swung open, Nelson dug his spurs into War Paint's shoulders, just as the rules of bronc riding require. The horse hurtled out of the chute. He punctuated his second leap with a furious kick of his hind legs, jerking his rider forward out of the saddle. On the pinto's third jump—the infamous one that sent most riders sprawling—Nelson was already halfway through a swan dive to the ground. As the champion cowboy rolled in the dust, the champion bucking horse jackknifed across the area in a boisterous dance of triumph. War Paint had needed only two seconds to prove who was the better rodeo performer—the champion of champions.

War Paint came naturally by his unruly disposition. Foaled in the early 1940s among the wild horse herds of southwestern Oregon, he spent the first few years of his life running free. He was captured during an annual roundup by the Klamath Indians and owned briefly by a Klamath rancher, Orrie

Summers, who named him Chemulwick, the Klamath word for "painted horse."

In 1951, Summers sold the pinto to Hank and Bobby Christensen, stock contractors from Eugene who provided bucking horses for rodeos. They changed his name to War Paint, and he went on to become one of the greatest saddle broncs of his time. Some claimed he could buck off nine of ten riders.

For the next fifteen years, War Paint followed the rodeo circuit to Denver, Pendleton, Cheyenne, and cow towns in between. He soon earned a reputation as an honest, consistent bucker with a "belly full of bed springs."

"He bucked you off fair and square," according to Bobby Christensen Jr., who grew up watching War Paint perform. "He didn't whirl or rear."

Renowned bronc rider Casey Tibbs was humbled more than once by the big, showy pinto. "He's a horse that allows you no mistakes," the cowboy once said. "If you ride him, you'll win the money every time—he's that tough. But if your spurs hang just a split second in his neck or if your weight gets just an ounce too far to one side, he'll fling you clear out of the arena."

Tibbs was the man who, at the end of the 1956 rodeo season, first came up with the idea of choosing a bucking horse of the year. The top ten saddle bronc riders voted, and War Paint was the first horse ever to receive the honor, presented by the Professional Rodeo Cowboys Association. He was selected from among an estimated 2,500 saddle broncs performing in professional rodeos that year. Most of the men who voted for him knew what it felt like to part from his saddle. War Paint went on to win the award in 1957 and 1958.

Outside of the rodeo arena, War Paint acquired a less desirable reputation.

"He was an outlaw," said the younger Bobby Christensen. "When he was young, he was pretty much treacherous. You wanted to be careful when you worked around him. . . . He didn't like people too well."

Bob Cook, secretary for the Christensen Brothers' outfit, once described War Paint to *The Western Horseman* magazine like this: "War Paint is a champion every inch of the way. He is smart and looks for every advantage. Mostly, War Paint is an easy horse to handle, but he can't be trusted. If he happens to get mad or upset, he is apt to kick, paw, and bite. . . . War Paint pretty well runs the headquarters-ranch horse pasture and the barnyard. He will contentedly eat and drink with the other horses until he decided that one of them is a little too close, or getting a little too familiar. On these occasions, he will run all of the other horses off. They go, too, and real quick-like."

■ ■ ■

War Paint retired in 1964, but even in his last year on the rodeo circuit, he gave cowboys an intimidating ride. By 1975, he was old, blind, and arthritic, so the Christensens thought it best to have him put to death. With their permission, Pendleton rancher Kent Rothrock had the gelding's body mounted in a bucking position and presented it to the Pendleton Round-Up Hall of Fame, where it quickly became the most popular exhibit. The three-time champ is still there today, kicking up his heels in a challenge to folks who dare to think her could be tamed.

Packy. Copyright Oregon Zoo, photo by Michael Duham

Packy
Premier
Pachyderm

"You can't put a price on the affection the people of Portland feel for Belle and their baby [Packy]. To lose them would be like losing one of your own children."

—SAVE THE ELEPHANTS CAMPAIGN press release, April 27, 1962

"It's a boy!" the Portland *Oregonian* whooped in a page-one banner headline.

City residents had been waiting for months to hear this colossal news. Now, at last, their vigil was over, and the celebration had just begun. A local civic group hoisted a blue flag in honor of the blessed event. The birth attendants exchanged proud handshakes and weary grins, and the new father ate his congratulatory cigar.

At the Oregon Zoo on the west side of the city, the object of all this commotion tottered at his mother's side, unaware that he had just made history. In the early morning hours of

- 33 -

April 14, 1962, he had become the first elephant born in the Western Hemisphere in almost half a century. And his birth represented a jumbo step forward in the race to save his species from extinction.

The Great Portland Elephant Watch had kicked off in January 1962, when folks learned that Belle, one of five Asian elephants at the zoo, was eighteen months pregnant and 1,000 pounds heavier than her usual three tons. No one knew for sure when the baby was due—in fact, no one knew much of anything about elephant reproduction—so reporters, photographers, and zoo personnel camped out night and day at the elephant barn, determined not to miss the big event. A radio station began broadcasting hourly "Belle bulletins," and toy stores stuffed their shelves with stuffed pachyderms.

The people of Portland were infatuated with the prospect of having a little "Dumbo" to call their own. They swamped the zoo with phone calls and gifts, including an elephant-sized bouquet of 300 long-stemmed roses, presented by a local florist. Belle munched these appreciatively, swallowing the thorny stems and spitting out the blossoms. They were a nice change of pace from her usual daily diet of one and a half bales of timothy hay, three gallons of oats, six pounds of bread, fifty pounds of carrots, half a box of apples, twenty-five pounds of bananas, a quarter of a box of oranges, and ten pounds of freshly dug dirt, to help with digestion. Of course, Belle was eating for two. Like other expectant mothers, she also developed a few cravings during her pregnancy, including a taste for black coffee and empty film cartons.

As the big day approached, a team of six prepared as best they could to help the hefty mom-to-be through labor and delivery. None of the men—a veterinarian, an obstetrician, a cardiologist, the zoo director, the head elephant keeper, and an elephant trainer—knew a thing about delivering an infant elephant that would probably weigh as much as each of them did. For that matter, there wasn't a man or woman in North America who did. But some of them knew a great deal about elephants, and others had presided at the births of humans, lions, buffalo, and bears. Together, they were probably the best midwives that bulging Belle could ask for.

For weeks, the delivery team lounged in the hay in the smelly elephant barn turned maternity ward. They passed the time playing poker, using Belle's liver pills and antibiotic capsules for chips. And they nibbled away at one hundred pounds of peanuts, the gift of yet another local admirer.

On the ominous evening of Friday, the 13th of April, all was quiet on the elephant front. At midnight, veterinarian Matt Maberry checked on his lady-in-waiting and noticed nothing unusual. When less than an hour later he got an urgent phone call about a poisoned poodle, he set off across town to tend to his patient, fairly confident that no one would miss him. While he was treating the dog, he got another emergency call—this time from a zoo guard alarmed by a change in Belle's behavior. Maberry rushed back to the zoo to find the elephant well into labor.

Belle was bellowing oddly, tossing her head from side to side, and alternately standing and kneeling. Her eyes bulged with the strain of her contractions. A few minutes before six, she began whirling in circles, pivoting on her front feet. Two minutes later, a pair of hind feet emerged, and in seconds Belle's baby plopped to the floor in a discombobulated heap. It was the seventh elephant born and bred in North America since the arrival of the species by ship in

- 35 -

1796—and the first born since 1918. None of the others survived to maturity.

Like many new babies, this one was so homely he was cute. In the opinion of one observer, he looked like a fatigued anteater—a 225-pound one—and he squeaked like a leaky balloon.

An *Oregonian* reporter described him like this: "'Fuzzy-Face' looks like a mouse beside his three-ton mother. . . . He stands about three feet tall, is the color of mud and is covered with a long fuzz. He has a head of black hair, a miniature moustache and a beard. But the hair on his legs and body is blondish.

"His tail is longer than his trunk. His eyes are bigger than his appetite, red-rimmed but brown like his mother's. He is altogether ridiculous, but obviously the apple of his mother's eye."

■ ■ ■

Belle's birth attendants weren't sure how the new mother would react to her "little" bundle of joy. After all, she had never witnessed a birth, let alone given birth herself. Did she understand what was happening to her? Would her maternal instinct kick into gear when at last she beheld her baby?

At first, the watching men had their doubts. As soon as the infant appeared, Belle turned and gave a couple of swift kicks to its wrinkled rear. The men were about to rush in to save the calf when they realized Belle was doing what any good doctor would. She was spanking her baby to help him start breathing.

Within thirty hours of the birth, folks began flocking to the zoo to visit Belle and her son. Ten thousand well-wishers showed up on Sunday to crowd onto the viewing patio at the elephant barn. The following weekend, almost 40,000 swarmed through the gates, setting a new zoo attendance record. One man claimed he stood in line for an hour and forty-five minutes to get a five-minute glimpse of the pair—not that he was complaining.

A local radio station held a citywide contest to choose a name for the little fellow. Packy won out over Belle Boy, Ding Dong, and Nogero (that's Oregon spelled backwards).

Two days after Packy's birth, Portland got news that burst its celebratory balloon. Belle's owner, Morgan Berry, had been besieged by offers to buy the pair. A professional animal importer and trainer from the Seattle area, he had been boarding Belle at the zoo each winter since 1960, along with two other elephants, including Packy's father, Thonglaw.

"I'd like to leave them here," he told a reporter regretfully. "I like Portland. . . . But I have to make a living."

The city was not about to give up its newest celebrities without a fight. When Berry agreed to sell the elephants to the city if it could come up with $30,000 within two weeks, officials promptly launched a "Save the Elephants" campaign and solicited donations.

Portlanders found all kinds of imaginative ways to cough up the cash. School children contributed pennies, matched by their teachers. Businesses passed the hat among their employees. The city parks department sponsored a peanut-rolling benefit in which kids raced to push peanuts with their noses, and firefighters scattered more than a thousand donation-collection cans around town. Various organizations sponsored a bowling tournament, a square-dance contest, and a "Belle ball."

On May Day, Portlanders awoke to find a welcome surprise on their doorstep. Not only had they raised enough money to buy Belle and Packy, but Berry had decided to throw in his other two elephants, Thonglaw and Pet, free of charge, rather than break up the "happy herd."

It was a whopping bargain, the *Oregonian* pointed out— more than 20,000 pounds of elephant at less than $1.50 a pound! It was also the beginning of a unique breeding program that would result in twenty-six more elephant births— making Portland the unofficial "Elephant Capital of the World." The program not only has boosted the population of the endangered Asian elephant, it has yielded crucial knowledge about breeding that may help to preserve the species in the wild. The city also is the primary supplier of calves to zoos throughout the United States.

Today, six elephants make their homes at the Oregon Zoo, and they continue to be the most popular animals on exhibit. In recent years, visitors have also been treated to an unusual display of elephant art. Using their trunks to blow fingerpaints or to hold a brush, the elephants have created masterpieces that would do Jackson Pollock proud. One such painting sold for $1,300.

Some critics have questioned in recent years whether zoos should keep elephants, which are high-maintenance animals. One particular problem is that they are prone to chronic foot ailments unless they can walk many miles in a day—something that's tough to do in a zoo. The Oregon Zoo responded by researching and finding solutions to the problem, including installing a rubberized floor that helps the elephants avoid deadly foot injuries and disease.

Today, the elephants are doing fine. The undisputed master of the herd continues to be Packy, who at ten feet tall and 13,000 pounds is now the largest known Asian elephant in the world. Middle-aged at forty-two, he's fathered seven calves of his own.

Packy's birthday is an annual event that draws as many as 10,000 people to the zoo. Guests don paper elephant ears, sing to the world-renowned birthday boy, and watch as he's served his own special cake—a thirty-five-pound concoction made with whole wheat and bran, slathered with peanut-butter frosting, and topped with carrot "candles." Depending on his mood, Packy's been known either to shovel his treat into his mouth in giant chunks or stomp it to smithereens.

Either way, he's one of the best presents the Oregon Zoo ever received.

A 1981 photo of Pete and owner Laurie. *Medford Mail Tribune*

Pete
The Cat's Meow

"'Meow' is like 'Aloha'—it can mean anything."

—HANK KETCHUM, American cartoonist

Pete Scott's welcome to Hollywood was suitable for a star: swarming reporters, popping flashbulbs, and a limousine ride to a posh suite at the Beverly Wilshire Hotel. It was all a bit overwhelming for a guy who was perfectly happy with a bowl of milk and a catnap in the sun.

So what catapulted nine-year-old Pete from obscurity to stardom? That tale begins back in 1981 with a box of cat food and a bit of luck.

As a kitten, some catastrophe had robbed poor Pete of a home. So the sleek black tom with lemon-drop eyes had parked on the porch of the Scott family in Ocean City, New Jersey, and waited for them to realize how lucky they were he'd come along. Long before the Scotts moved to Central Point, Oregon, in 1980, Pete had padded his way into their hearts and settled there for good.

By 1981, Pete was a ponderous twenty-two pounds—a victim of middle-age spread. He'd obviously made it a point never to miss a meal. One day, as Shirley Scott was filling his bowl with Meow Mix, she noticed a contest entry form printed on the back of the box. The manufacturer, Ralston Purina, was conducting a search for the feline with the most marvelous meow. The grand prize was $25,000 and the chance to star in a TV commercial for the kibbles that cool cats "ask for by name."

Pete had always been a talkative fellow, so on a whim Shirley entered him in the contest. She was flabbergasted when she learned that he was one of six regional finalists. His name had been drawn at random from more than 100,000 entries. Soon the Scotts were packing for a week-long, all-expense paid trip to Beverly Hills, where Pete would compete in the final round of the Ralston Purina Meow Off.

The trip to California was a fun-filled holiday for the human members of the Scott clan. Shirley, her husband, Bernard, and her daughter, Laurie, flitted from Disneyland to Marineland, from Knott's Berry Farm to Universal Studios. They even got tickets to a taping of *The Tonight Show* with Johnny Carson. Meanwhile, Pete lounged alone in his hotel room, resting his vocal cords for the big event.

On their second day in Beverly Hills, the Scotts got a chance to scout the competition. In order to avoid any last-minute stage fright, the contest sponsors had decided to pre-record the cat calls and play them for the judges later.

Pete was the oldest of the competitors, but the classiest was definitely Elsa, a purebred, blue-point Himalayan in the advanced stages of pregnancy. (She would later be disqualified when she went into labor and had kittens.)

Like Pete, the other contenders were average, everyday house cats. There was Angelo, a black alley cat who'd come all the way from Rhode Island; Fred, a black and white shorthair who looked a little like Charlie Chaplin; Molly, a five-year-old part-Persian and part who-knows-what-else; and Little Thomas Moore, a kitten whose litter mates were all named Thomas because their owners couldn't tell them apart. Fortunately for these commoners, pedigree didn't count. The judges would base their decision solely on the quality of the meow.

Finally, on August 12, 1981, it was time to let the winning cat out of the bag. Feline fanciers filed into the Persian Room of the Beverly Hills Hotel until the place was packed so full there wasn't room to swing a cat. The five contestants crouched nervously in their cat carriers as the celebrity judges—Dick Van Patten, Jo Anne Worley, Louis Nye, and Pamela Mason—settled into their seats at the front of the room. There was a brief hush, then the tap rolled, and the caterwauling began.

After what seemed like an ear-splitting eternity, the judges agreed on a top cat, and Pete was their pick of the litter. He'd licked the competition by a vote of four to one with a yowl that one judge described as "something right out of the jungle." Another praised Pete for having "the strongest, truest meow—an appealing meow that was distinct and unique." Who ever said that black cats are nothing but bad luck?!

Pete's fame quickly made headlines all across the nation. He appeared on a Los Angeles TV talk show and was featured on National Public Radio's *All Things Considered*. Newspapers big and small carried the story of the celebrity cat from Central Point. Pete even began to get fan mail, including a letter from a Medford, Oregon, woman who offered her pet Missy's paw in marriage.

The Scotts, meanwhile, were planning how to spend Pete's winnings. They set the bulk of the money aside for sixteen-year-old Laurie's college education. But they didn't forget from whence their windfall came. They donated $1,000 to the Southern Oregon Humane Society in honor of good old Pete.

Pete never did make his television debut.

When the Scotts learned that their pet would have to spend a month in California learning how to act in the Meow Mix commercial, Shirley decided that, in this case, the price of fame was too high. The world would just have to limp along to the sound of some lesser cat's song.

"We thought it would be too hard for him to be away from us," she said. "I think he would have been homesick."

So Pete slipped out of the spotlight and back into his favorite porch chair. Maybe his naps were filled with dreams of the day he was the ultimate cat's meow.

Bob
Forecasting Phenomenon

"Everybody kids me that most people carry around their grandchildren's pictures, but I carry Bob the Weather Cat. He has made a difference in my life. Some people might think it's silly, but I don't."

—AN ELDERLY PORTLAND WOMAN quoted in
Cats Magazine, July 1988

It often rains cats and dogs on the Pacific Coast, but only in Portland has a cat reigned. His name was Bob, and his interest in the weather was what catapulted him from back-alley stray to king of local television.

Bob's tale is a classic rags-to-riches story. It began in 1983, when he was a homeless waif fishing tidbits from garbage cans and fleeing BB guns and nasty dogs. His fortunes changed when he pussyfooted into the yard of Bob and Sheilagh Foster, compassionate cat-lovers who coaxed him

- 45 -

Bob the weather cat dressed as Uncle Sam. Copyright 1986 Robert Louis Foster, Uncle Sam hat made by Sheilagh Fay Conroy

into making their home his own. In the beginning, they called him Hank, but he would be remembered by most Oregonians as Bob the Weather Cat.

For three years, Bob lived like any ordinary housecat, lounging in sunny windows and catnapping in easy chairs. But as so often happens, his destiny changed course in one twitch of a cat's whisker.

Bob's new guardian—the bigger one with the deeper voice—was a cameraman for Portland's KATU television station, and one of his responsibilities was to provide appropriate videotape to serve as a backdrop for the evening weather forecasts. On rainy days, he'd shoot folks with umbrellas; on sunny days, he'd shoot flowers.

On one of the latter, he was focusing his camera on a spray of blossoms in his backyard when Bob—the smaller one with the longer whiskers—sauntered over to investigate and horned his way into the picture. Bob the Human rather liked the effect, so that week Bob the Cat made his television debut, though it was just as an anonymous backdrop.

About a week later, Jeff Gianola, the KATU weatherman at the time, suggested that Foster feature Bob in his videotape again. The cameraman complied, but when Gianola introduced the shot on the air, he couldn't remember his new co-star's name. Instead of Hank, he called the hefty tom Bob the Weather Cat, knowing that he belonged to Bob Foster, and from then on, Bob it was. A gray and white star had been born, complete with his very own stage name.

For the next seven years, Bob the Weather Cat was a regular feature of Friday forecasts, and Foster began dressing him in costumes to reflect the weather or to signify holidays and other special occasions. He appeared in earmuffs and a scarf when snow was predicted and doll-sized sunglasses when it was hot, as Santa "Claws" at Christmas and as Uncle Sam on the Fourth of July. He wore bunny ears at Easter and a cowboy hat during the Pendleton rodeo, a green bow tie on St. Patrick's Day and a formal tux when the Broadway show *Cats* came to town.

Bob resisted the costumes at first, but eventually he condescended, recognizing, perhaps, that sacrifices must sometimes be made for the sake of art. In fact, Foster once noted, "he usually purred when I dressed him." It would take much more than foolish attire to ruffle this cool cat's fur.

Sheilagh Foster made most of the outfits Bob wore on the air, but fans from across the nation soon began contributing to his wardrobe as well. As a result, the silky celebrity never wore the same thing twice.

Bob was an immediate hit with KATU viewers. People began setting their VCRs every Friday night to record his two-minute appearances. The famous feline was so deluged with fan mail that the Fosters rented a post-office box just for him. They also served as his secretaries—answering every note on the cat's own letterhead stationery. There were Bob bumper stickers and buttons, posters and greeting cards. He was featured in *Cats, People,* and *National Geographic World* magazines, and he received gifts from as far away as Massachusetts and Canada, from tourists who were smitten with him while vacationing in Oregon.

"Those people out there . . . who watch him every Friday are wonderful," Sheilagh Foster once said. "We get letters from people who say, 'I am a widow. I used to have nothing in life to look forward to and now on Fridays I look forward to being with Bob.'"

Co-workers at KATU learned the extent of Bob's popularity in 1986, when his appearance was canceled because it was deemed too lighthearted to accompany a tidal-wave warning. "By seven o'clock the switchboard was jammed," a station employee recalled. "One lady said, 'I just want you to know you ruined my evening because I invited six couples over for a Bob party.'"

To everyone's surprise, Bob had become a forecasting phenomenon, known and loved for his quiet dignity. One weatherman called him the John Wayne of catdom, while some of his competitors tended to get a little catty.

"He's had no impact on us," groused the weather forecaster at another Portland station. "Channel 2 is so far behind us in the ratings, I'm sure the cat hasn't helped them one bit."

Some of Bob's co-workers were bemused and humbled by his success. "You really have to keep your ego in check," said one KATU anchorman, "when you realize a cat is getting more mail than you."

Still, the former foundling never let fame go to his head. When he wasn't filming, he prowled his neighborhood unrecognized, stalking birds and chasing leaves like any ordinary cat. And like many a celebrity, he made benefit appearances for charities, including the Oregon Humane Society.

Bob's reign came to a tragic end in 1993, when he was diagnosed with liver cancer and mercifully put to sleep. He was estimated to be thirteen years old at the time.

When KATU announced the death, its switchboard was flooded with condolence calls—twenty-five an hour the operator estimated. Some callers asked whether there would be a memorial service and where they could send donations and flowers. One viewer confessed, "I hate cats, but I loved Bob." Outside the station, someone posted a sign reading PORTLAND SALUTES BOB THE WEATHER CAT. WE'LL MISS YOU BOB.

It was hard to imagine anyone filling Bob's big paws, but the Fosters had an understudy waiting in the wings—a laid-back, black and white tom. When KATU sponsored a "televote" to name the new guy, more than 69,000 people called in—a tribute, in part, to Bob's memory. The winning name was Tom—not very creative but it was his real name after all, and it was a bit more dignified than the second-place choice, Bubba.

After Tom had been on the air three years, the station's new news director called Foster into his office. "Bob," he said, "that new cat just doesn't have that on-air charisma that the other one did, so I've decided to take him off the air. I'll answer all the complaints."

"Well," Bob the Human replied, "after 560 or so cos-tumes I could give it a rest."

Tom didn't seem to mind either. Perhaps he realized that Bob the Weather Cat was an awfully tough act to follow.

Still, everyone knows that bit about cats having nine lives, so Bob fans may want to stay tuned. Portland's most famous feline may be back for his second go-round—same time, same station.

Keiko
Ailing Orca

"[Orcas] are king of beasts. We consider
ourselves rulers of the world, but in
the marine part of it, for many more
millions of years than we've been
around, they've been the top dog."

—KEN BALCOMB, Center for Whale Research, quoted in
The Oregonian, October 3, 1994

*The restive killer whale patrolled its cramped pool like a lion pacing
its cage. Once part of a formidable tribe that ruled the Icelandic seas,
it was now nothing more than a court jester, performing acrobatic
stunts at a marine park to earn its daily meals. There were some people who deplored its plight and thought it should be free.*

If that sounds like the sentimental plot of the 1993
movie, *Free Willy,* you're right. But it also became the open-
ing act of a real-life drama with the same star cast in the lead:
a killer whale known off-screen as Keiko (KAY-ko). Keiko
became one of the most famous marine mammals in the
world, and he made Oregon the first stop on a difficult journey home to the wild.

Keiko. Chris Schmitz

Keiko's tale of woe began about 1980, when he was captured by a commercial whaler off the coast of Iceland. He was sold first to an aquarium in Ontario and then, in 1985, to Reino Aventura, a theme park in Mexico City. It was there that he was discovered by a pair of movie producers who cast him in the title role of *Free Willy,* a Warner Brothers film about a troubled boy who befriends a captive killer whale and schemes to set him free.

In real life, too, Keiko needed a savior. After his capture, he grew into a 25-foot-long, 7,000-pound behemoth, far too big for his tank at Reino Aventura. The tank's filtration system couldn't keep up with the amount of body waste Keiko produced, so the water became filthy. It also was far too warm for his arctic tastes. As a result, Keiko developed a nasty skin disease, and his dorsal fin drooped, perhaps from lack of exercise. Bored and frustrated, he wore down his teeth gnawing at the concrete walls of his pool. And giant though he was, marine biologists estimated that he was one to two tons underweight compared to healthy males of his species. They predicted he could die quickly if his living conditions weren't improved.

For years, Keiko's owners tried to find a more suitable home for their star attraction. The whale's trainer at Reino Aventura called him "cute, sweet, [and] very curious," but other aquariums were leery about taking him because of his health problems. Ironically, it was in part Keiko's skin condition—visible to savvy movie-goers as wartlike lumps around his tail and flippers—that led to concerted efforts to turn his life around. After the release of *Free Willy,* its producers, Richard Donner and Lauren Shuler-Donner, received tens of thousands of letters from animal lovers distressed by Keiko's fate. The writers demanded that Keiko, like Willy, be freed.

The Donners needed little convincing. They, too, were disturbed by the idea of keeping such an intelligent and elegant animal confined to an aquatic prison. So they turned for advice to Earth Island Institute, a California-based nonprofit organization dedicated to the preservation of marine life. They asked the institute to help form a plan to move Keiko to a better facility. Eventually, yet another would-be rescuer joined the team: Ken Balcomb, founder and director of the Center for Whale Research in Washington state.

Together, Keiko's new friends conceived an imaginative scenario. With $2 million in seed money contributed by Warner Brothers, they established the Free Willy Foundation and launched a major fundraising campaign. They raised millions more in order to transfer Keiko to a roomier pen in Oregon where he could convalesce and relearn the skills he needed to survive in the wild.

After an intensive continent-wide search, the group settled on the Oregon Coast Aquarium in Newport, a three-year-old nonprofit facility with a strong emphasis on education, research, and conservation. With the foundation's blessing and financing, the aquarium constructed a $7.3-million, state-of-the-art whale pool more than four times as large as Keiko's old home in Mexico. It held two million gallons of cold seawater pumped from nearby Yaquina Bay and was "landscaped" with natural rock. In early 1996, Keiko was moved to the pool.

Keiko, whose name means "Lucky One" in Japanese, was fed about 300 pounds of fish a day. He drew more than two and a half million visitors during the thirty-two months he rehabilitated at the aquarium.

In all, about $10 million was spent on the pool and getting Keiko ready to be freed. That might seem like a lot, but as Mark Berman, a spokesman for Earth Island Institute, pointed out, "this facility will not just be for Keiko and then be an empty tank. It will be a rescue center for unwanted marine animals that have no other place to go," such as dolphins and whales that wash up on beaches or are orphaned by aquariums that no longer want them.

"Keiko is just a symbol of the many whales and dolphins who've suffered at the hands of humans," Berman said.

Killer whales are not actually whales at all but are the largest members of the dolphin family. Like the common dolphin, they're mammals rather than fish, and so they breathe air. Killer whales are also called orcas.

The importance of family to the orca can hardly be overstated. In fact, some researchers believe it may be the most socially bonded species on earth. Each animal lives in a basic, matriarchal social unit called a sub-pod, made up of a mother, an adult son, and her adult daughters and their offspring. Because of the importance of family to orcas, Keiko's rescuers located Keiko's original pod, or family group, off the coast of Iceland, near where he had originally been captured. Genetic studies showed that the pod was Keiko's birth "community." The plan was to return the captive star to the open sea and the company of his kin.

"The moms and the females lead the pack," researcher Balcomb said. "Even though you may have a male out in front, that doesn't mean he is calling the shots. His mother is there. If his mother turns, he'll turn, too."

In the natural scheme of things, orca calves don't leave their mothers, and researchers have found no evidence of a killer whale transferring permanently from one pod to another. Marine biologists believed Keiko had little chance of surviving in the wild without rejoining his native pod.

In captivity, orcas usually have an average lifespan of ten years, while in the wild males live an average of about thirty

- 55 -

years and females fifty. Keiko was about twenty years old when, in the fall of 1998, he was airlifted to a pen in the chilly waters of the North Atlantic Ocean off Iceland. His handlers went to work preparing him to again live in the wild. They taught him to catch live fish on his own so he wouldn't depend on humans for his food.

Almost four years later, Keiko was released from the pen. He swam straight for Norway, some 900 miles away. There he slipped into Taknes Bay, a deep slit of coastal water that doesn't freeze in winter. Keepers fed him and led him from small boats on "walks" around the fjords so he could keep in shape. Keiko also could roam freely, something he would do at night. But Keiko still seemed to want to be around humans, and he sometimes let fans pet him and even crawl on his back.

On December 12, 2003, Keiko fans around the world were saddened to learn that the famous killer whale had died after suddenly becoming ill with pneumonia. At the age of about twenty-seven, Keiko was relatively old for an orca in captivity.

David Phillips, executive director of the San Francisco–based Free Willy-Keiko Foundation, said that, while Keiko's death was sad, his life helped the public understand how to deal with captive orcas. "We took the hardest candidate and took him from near death in Mexico to swimming with wild whales in Norway," he said. "Keiko proved a lot of naysayers wrong and that this can work, and that is a very powerful thing."

Mark Collson, a board member of the Oregon Coast Aquarium, said Keiko had a powerful effect on people around the globe. "I once I had a friend describe him as a 4,000-pound golden retriever," Collson said. "He was like the family dog; he wanted to be next to you."

Bibliography

Seaman: Expedition Mascot

Blumberg, Rhonda. *The Incredible Journey of Lewis & Clark.* New York: Scholastic, Inc., 1987.

Charbonneau, Louis. "Seaman's Trail: Fact vs. Fiction," *We Proceeded On,* journal of the Lewis and Clark Trail Heritage Foundation, November 1989.

Clarke, Charles G. *The Men of the Lewis and Clark Expedition.* Glendale, Calif.: The Aurthur H. Clark Co., 1970.

DeVoto, Bernard, ed. *The Journals of Lewis and Clark.* Boston: Houghton Mifflin Co., 1953.

Jackson, Donald. "A Dog Named Scannon—Until Recently," in *Among the Sleeping Giants: Occasional Pieces on Lewis and Clark.* Urbana: University of Illinois Press, 1987.

LaGow, Bette. "The Nanny," *Dog Fancy Magazine,* August 1994. (This article is about the Newfoundland breed.)

Lewis, Meriwether. *The Lewis and Clark Expedition.* Vol. 3. Philadelphia: J. B. Lippincott Co., 1961. Originally published 1814.

Osgood, Ernest S. "Our Dog Scannon: Partner in Discovery," *Montana, the Magazine of Western History,* Summer 1976.

Reelfoot: Outlaw Grizzly

Bean, Fred. Interview with KDRV-TV, Medford, Ore., April 10, 1990. (Fred Bean is Purl Bean's son.)

Nielson, Carole. "'Reel' Bear of a Tale," *Wild West Magazine,* October 1993.

"Reel Foot on Exhibition," *The Democratic Times,* Medford, Ore., July 11, 1890.

Schrader, George R. "The Grizzly Bear of California," *Siskiyou Pioneer,* 1946.

Vincent, Dale. "Death of Siskiyou's Old Reelfoot," undated, unpublished manuscript on file at Southern Oregon Historical Society, Medford, Ore. (George Wright was Bill Wright's nephew.)

Bobbie: Cross-Country Canine

Alexander, Charles. *Bobbie: A Great Collie.* New York: Dodd, Mead & Co., 1926.

Ames, Felicia. "What Is That Incredible Sixth Sense Dogs Seem to Have?" *Family Weekly,* February 18, 1973.

"Bobbie to Enter the Movie World," *The Silverton Appeal,* May 2, 1924.

Brazier, G. F., "Bobbie—The Wonder Dog of Oregon," in *Animal Pals,* ed. by Curtis Wager-Smith. Philadelphia: Macrae Smith Co., 1932.

———. Letters on file at the Oregon Historical Society, Portland.

"Dog Feted in Portland," *The Silverton Appeal,* April 11, 1924.

"Dog Returns After Long Trip," *The Silverton Appeal,* February 22, 1924.

Greene, Lorne. "Lost and Found," in *The Lorne Greene Book of Remarkable Animals.* New York: Simon & Schuster, 1980.

Paulson, Dusty. Employee of Silverton Market Garden. Telephone interview on November 1, 2004.

"Remembering Bobbie the Wonder Dog," *Animal Focus,* newsletter of the Oregon Humane Society, Winter 1988.

War Paint: Buckin' Champ

Armstrong, Jerry. "Picked Up in the Rodeo Arena," *The Western Horseman,* July 1958.

———. "Picked Up in the Rodeo Arena," *The Western Horseman,* March 1959.

Boley, Robert. "'Greatest of All' Bucks No More," *The Oregon Journal,* October 10, 1969.

"Bucking Horse of the Year Trophy Awarded to 'War Paint' at Denver," *Rodeo Sports News,* February 1, 1958.

Christensen, Bobby, Jr. Telephone interview, July 14, 1995.

Crider, Bob. "Famous Bucking Horse Returns to R-Up," *East Oregonian,* Pendleton, September 14, 1976.

"Famed Horse to Stay in R-Up Hall of Fame," *East Oregonian,* Pendleton, December 1, 1977.

Sweek, Jack C. President of Pendleton Round-Up Hall of Fame, Letter to author, June 21, 1995.

"Today's Greatest Bucking Horse War Paint Honored," *The Horse Lover's Magazine,* February/March 1958.

Packy: Premier Pachyderm

Alexander, Shana. "Belle's Baby-225 Pounds and All Elephant," *Life,* May 11, 1962.

Cohen, Steve. Public relations officer at Metro Washington Park Zoo, Portland. Telephone interview, June 7, 1995.

D'Ae-Smith, Linda. Public relations specialist at Oregon Zoo. E-mail message, December 21, 2004.

"Drive to Buy Elephants Gaining City Momentum," *The Oregonian,* Portland, April 26, 1962.

"Elephant Fans Jam Zoo, Donate $1,200 to Fund," *The Oregonian,* Portland, April 24, 1962.

"Expectant Elephant," *Newsweek,* February 5, 1962.

Hauser, Susan G. "Seven Tons of Birthday Fun," *Wall Street Journal,* April 14, 1995.

"Keep the Elephants Drive Seeks Help," *The Oregonian,* Portland, April 17, 1962.

"Portland Zoo to Get Elephant Bonus Deal," *The Oregonian,* Portland, May 2, 1962.

Richards, Leverett, "It's a Boy for Big Belle at Portland Zoo," *The Sunday Oregonian,* Portland, April 15, 1962.

Tisdale, Sallie. "A Reporter at Large: The Only Harmless Great Thing," *The New Yorker,* January 23, 1989.

"Zoo May Lose Elephant Baby," *The Oregonian,* Portland, April 16, 1962.

Pete: The Cat's Meow

Lewellen, Judie. "Meow Off," *Us Magazine,* October 27, 1981.

"Pete Receives Fan Mail and None of It's Catty," *The Mail Tribune,* Medford, Oregon, August 21, 1981.

Scarbrough, Roy. "Local Cat in National Meow-Off," *The Mail Tribune,* Medford, Oregon, June 16, 1981.

———. "Pete Meows Way to National Championship," *The Mail Tribune,* Medford, Oregon, August 13, 1981.

Scott, Shirley. Telephone interview, August 4, 1995.

"Six Cats to Match Meows for $25,000 Prize . . . ," press release issued by Ralston Purina Co., July 20, 1981.

Bob: Forecasting Phenomenon

"Bob the Weather Cat's Fans to be Offered KATU Tribute," *The Oregonian,* Portland, March 11, 1993.

Foster, Bob. Bob's owner and photographer for KATU, Portland, Oregon. Interviews on November 23 and December 19, 2004.

Franzen, Robin. "Bob: The Weather Cat," *Cats Magazine,* July 1988.

Henniger, Jean. "Bob the Cat's Out of the Bag, into Fans' Hearts," *The Oregonian,* Portland, July 9, 1986.

Mahar, Ted. "Bob the Weather Cat Dies at 13," *The Oregonian,* Portland, March 10, 1993.

"Pretty Cool Cat," *National Geographic World,* August 1987.

Schulberg, Pete. "Viewers Show They Really Loved that Bob," *The Oregonian,* Portland, March 15, 1993.

"Willard Scott May Someday Feel Heat from a Frisky Competitor—Oregon's Bob the Weather Cat," *People Magazine,* July 18, 1988.

Keiko: Ailing Orca

Berman, Mark. Program associate with Earth Island Institute, San Francisco. Telephone interview, July 27, 1995.

Frank, Gerry. "Whale of a Time a Shoo-In in Warner Bros. Proposal," *The Oregonian,* Portland, September 9, 1994.

The Free Willy News, publication of the Free Willy Foundation, Vol. 1, 1995.

"'Free Willy' whale, Keiko, dies," cnn.com, December 13, 2003.

"'Free Willy' Whale Dies," *Associated Press,* December 13, 2003.

Gordon, David G., and Chuck Flaherty. *Field Guide to the Orca.* Seattle: Sasquatch Books, 1990.

Hammond, Diane. Public relations officer, Oregon Coast Aquarium, Newport.

"Keiko—The Long Effort for a Return Home," *Ocean Alert,* publication of Earth Island Institute, Winter/Spring 1995.

"Keiko to Move to Oregon," *Ocean Alert,* Summer/Fall 1995.

McDaniel, Jo Beth. "Won't Somebody Please Save This Whale?" *Life,* November 1993.

Meehan, Brian T. "Killer Whale Country," *The Oregonian,* Portland, October 3, 1994.

"Move Afoot to Move Willy," *The New York Times Magazine,* March 12, 1995.

"Movie's Star May Be Coming to State," *The Oregonian,*
Portland, November 30, 1994.

"The Whale's Tale," *People,* August 9, 1993.

Wise, James. "Killer Digs," *The Oregonian,* Portland, July 3,
1995.

About the Author

Gayle C. Shirley has written a dozen nonfiction books for children and young adults, including *M is for Montana, More than Petticoats: Remarkable Montana Women,* and *Charlie's Trail: The Life and Art of C. M. Russell.* This book is part of a series she has written about animal legends from throughout the West. She also has written articles for magazines such as *Boy's Life* and *Big Sky Journal.*

Gayle grew up in Colorado and Idaho and graduated from the University of Montana with a degree in journalism. She worked as a reporter and editor for daily Montana newspapers and as an editor for a publishing company before writing her first book. She is currently the public information officer for the Montana Department of Public Health and Human Services. She lives with her husband, Steve, and sons, Colin and Jesse, in Helena, Montana.

THE INSIDER'S SOURCE

With more than 540 West-related titles, we have the area covered. Whether you're looking for the path less traveled, a favorite place to eat, family-friendly fun, a breathtaking hike, or enchanting local attractions, our pages are filled with ideas to get you from one state to the next.

For a complete listing of all our titles, please visit our Web site at www.GlobePequot.com. The Globe Pequot Press is the largest publisher of local travel books in the United States and is a leading source for outdoor recreation guides.

FOR BOOKS TO THE WEST

Available wherever books are sold.
Orders can also be placed on the Web at www.GlobePequot.com, by phone from 8:00 A.M. to 5:00 P.M. at 1-800-243-0495, or by fax at 1-800-820-2329.

HOW TO
TALK
to
ANYONE
AT WORK

Avoid Awkwardness, Banish Social Anxiety,
and Achieve Your Greatest Professional
Goals WITHOUT Acting Fake

CARL WOLFE

 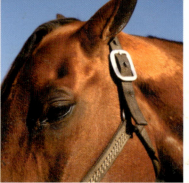 

heroic courageous swift **mighty** wily faithful sacred ferocious courageous mighty faithful ferocious heroic swift mighty **wily** faithful sacred ferocious heroic **courageous** swift mighty wily sacred ferocious heroic courageous swift mighty faithful sacred ferocious heroic courageous **swift** mighty wily faithful **sacred** ferocious heroic courageous swift mighty wily sacred ferocious heroic courageous swift mighty wily **faithful** sacred **ferocious** heroic

Legendary Tales . . . of Legends with Tails

Think all animals are created equal? Think again! **Amazing Animals of Oregon** features eight true tales about Oregon's most unforgettable animals, past and present, including a cross-country canine, outlaw grizzly, clever cat, and premier pachyderm. Look inside to discover what set these not-to-be-forgotten creatures apart from the pack—or sleuth, or clutter, or herd—and made them legends in Beaver State history.

Inside you'll meet:

- Bobbie—the homesick dog that traveled 3,000 miles across eight states to be reunited with his owners
- Reelfoot—the notorious outlaw grizzly whose deadly deeds brought his own demise
- Bob—the Portland feline that became a weather-forecasting phenomenon

$9.95
ISBN 0-7627-3856-1

P.O. Box 480
Guilford, CT 06437
www.InsidersGuide.com

Insiders' Guide® is an imprint of
The Globe Pequot Press

Cover photos © Getty Images
Cover design by Linda R. Loiewski